14.20

DATE DUE

MAY 2 4 2000	
AUG 1 5 2000	
OCT 2 0 2001	
DEC 1 7 2001	
APR 1 7 2002	
NOV 0 2 2002	
AUG 1 6 2004	
DEC 2 9 2004	
NOV 4 - 2006	
MAY 3 1 2008	

DEMCO, INC. 38-2931

JAN 0 4 1999

The United States

Montana

Paul Joseph
ABDO & Daughters

visit us at
www.abdopub.com

Published by Abdo & Daughters, 4940 Viking Drive, Suite 622, Edina, Minnesota 55435.
Copyright © 1998 by Abdo Consulting Group, Inc., Pentagon Tower, P.O. Box 36036, Minneapolis, Minnesota 55435 USA. International copyrights reserved in all countries. No part of this book may be reproduced in any form without written permission from the publisher.

Printed in the United States.

Cover and Interior Photo credits: Peter Arnold, Inc., Super Stock, Archive Photos

Edited by Lori Kinstad Pupeza
Contributing editor Brooke Henderson
Special thanks to our Checkerboard Kids—Jack Ward, Tyler Wagner, Peter Rengstorf, Morgan Roberts

All statistics taken from the 1990 census; The Rand McNally Discovery Atlas of The United States. Other sources: Compton's Encyclopedia, 1997, *Montana*, Heinrichs, Children's Press, Chicago, 1989.

Library of Congress Cataloging-in-Publication Data

Joseph, Paul, 1970-
        Montana / Paul Joseph.
        p. cm. -- (United States)
        Includes index.
        Summary: Examines the people, geography, history, and natural resources of the Treasure State.
        ISBN 1-56239-864-4
        1. Montana--Juvenile literature. [1. Montana.] I. Title. II. Series: United States (Series)
        F731.3.J67   1998   97-15206
        978.6--dc21   CIP
                                                             AC

Contents

Welcome to Montana

The name Montana comes from the Spanish word for mountain. But people in America call Montana the Treasure State. It is called the Treasure State because it has so many **minerals**, forests, and grazing lands.

The Treasure State is the national leader in the **mining** of gold, copper, silver, lead, and zinc. More sheep **graze** on Montana's land than most other states. The state also has Glacier and Yellowstone national parks.

Montana is a very big state. Only Alaska, Texas, and California are bigger in size. However, there are not very many people that live in the state. Only two cities in Montana have more than 50,000 people.

Montana does get a lot of visitors. **Tourism** is one of the biggest **industries** in the Treasure State. Because Montana is so beautiful and peaceful, many people go there on summer vacations. The number one place to visit in the state is Yellowstone National Park. Even in

the winter people visit Montana to ski and go to winter carnivals.

Glacier National Park, Montana.

Fast Facts

MONTANA

Capital
Helena (24,569 people)
Area
145,388 square miles
(376,553 sq km)
Population
803,655 people
Rank: 44th
Statehood
Nov. 8, 1889
(41st state admitted)
Principal rivers
Missouri River
Yellowstone River
Highest point
Granite Peak;
12,799 feet (3,901 m)
Largest city
Billings (81,151 people)
Motto
Oro y plata
(Gold and silver)
Song
"Montana"
Famous People
Gary Cooper, Will James, Mike
Mansfield, Jeannette Rankin,
Charles Russell

*S*tate Flag

*B*itterroot

*W*estern Meadowlark

*P*onderosa Pine

About Montana

The Treasure State

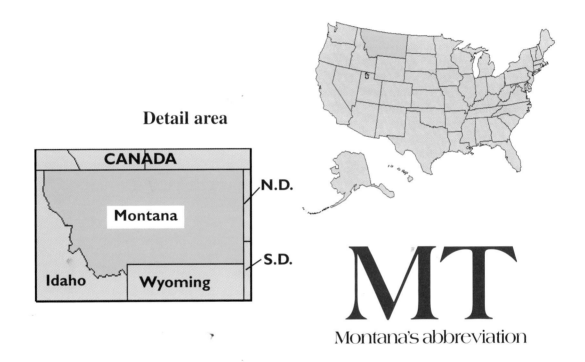

Detail area

CANADA

Montana

N.D.

S.D.

Idaho

Wyoming

MT
Montana's abbreviation

Borders: west (Idaho), north (Canada), east (North Dakota, South Dakota), south (Wyoming, Idaho)

Nature's Treasures

Montana has many treasures in its great state. In fact, there are so many that the state is called the Treasure State. There are lots of **minerals** in Montana's land. Long ago gold was often found. Today, the top minerals found are **petroleum**, **natural gas**, and coal.

Another treasure in Montana is the rich farmland. The state has about 22,000 farms and **ranches**. Montana produces wheat, hay, barley, and oats. The **vast grazing** areas feed many cows and sheep.

There are also millions of acres of forest in the Treasure State. Forests are filled with many different kinds of trees. Some of the trees that grow in Montana are the pine, western larch, fir, and spruce.

The wonderful scenery of the state brings millions of visitors each year. One of the best treasures of all is just being able to look out at the beautiful land.

Montana has rich farmland.

Beginnings

Dinosaurs once roamed Montana many millions of years ago. At one time the state was covered in huge glaciers of ice. This was known as the Ice Age. After it melted, Montana was left with deep forests, rivers, and mountains.

Native Americans were the first people to live in Montana. The Crow, Blackfeet, Sioux, Cheyenne, and Shoshone lived in Montana.

Lewis and Clark explored the state in 1805, and were among the first white men to enter the area. For the next 50 years, few people entered Montana, except for fur trappers and traders.

Then in 1858, gold was discovered at Gold Creek. **Settlers** started pushing to Montana by the hundreds. Almost overnight, towns sprang up in the state. The settlers started moving the Native Americans west and newcomers began taking over the state. Besides **mining**, the **settlers** started farming, **ranching**, and working with lumber.

The state became a dangerous place to live. Many outlaws came into the settlements to steal from and hurt people. In 1864, Congress created the Montana Territory. This helped to make law and order.

The Montana Territory was admitted to the Union 25 years later. On November 8, 1889, Montana became the 41st state. Helena was named the capital.

A gold miner in Montana.

B.C. to 1500s

 During the Ice Age, Montana is covered with glaciers.

 After the Ice Age, Montana is left with mountains, lakes, rivers, and forests.

 The first people to live in the land are the Crow, Blackfeet, Sioux, and Cheyenne.

Montana

B.C. to 1500s

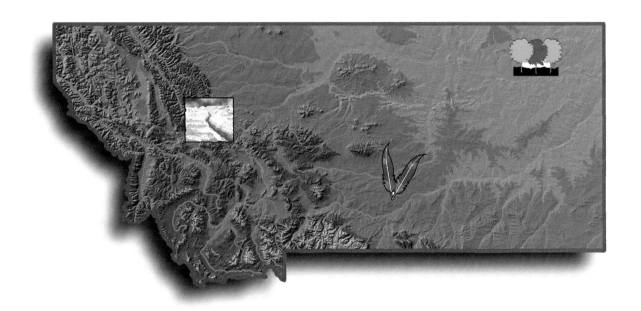

1700s to 1800s

 Early 1700s: French are allowed to trade fur in Montana.

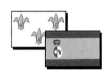 Late 1700s: Montana changes ownership many times, often between France and Spain.

 1805: Lewis and Clark cross Montana on the way to the Pacific Ocean.

 1862-1864: Gold is found at Gold Creek.

 1889: Montana becomes the 41st state on November 8. Helena is the capital.

Montana

1700s to 1800s

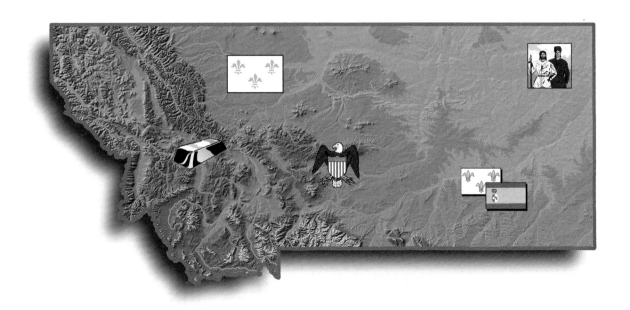

1900s

 1900s: Oil is discovered in Montana.

 1910: Glacier National Park is created.

 1916: Jeannette Rankin, from Montana, is the first United States congresswoman.

 1919-1926: A horrible drought ruins the farm land and its **crops**.

 1988: Montana suffers the worst drought since the 1920s. It is declared a drought disaster by the federal government.

Montana

1900s

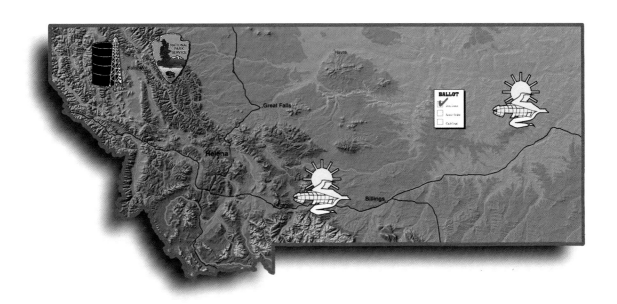

Montana's People

There are around 800,000 people in the state of Montana. It is the sixth smallest state in the country. **Native Americans** first lived on the land. Then there was a rush of **settlers** to the area when gold was discovered.

Although the state is small, many famous people have come from Montana. Gary Cooper was born in Helena, Montana. Cooper was a famous movie star from the 1930s to the 1950s.

A.B. Guthrie grew up in Choteau, Montana. He was a well-known writer. He wrote many books about the west and Montana. Montana is also called the "Big Sky Country," which is the name of a book he wrote.

Myrna Loy was born in Raidersburg, Montana. She was a popular actress from the 1920s to the 1950s. She was in more than 100 movies and starred in about 80 of those films.

Mike Mansfield served Montana in both the House and Senate in Congress. Later Mansfield was named ambassador to Japan.

Plenty Coups was a Crow Indian Chief. He was born near Billings, Montana, in 1848. He made the United States government pay his tribe for the land the government took from them. In 1921, he was made chief of all the Crow.

Today, many notable people vacation and have homes in Montana. Former Secretary of State James Baker has a **ranch** in Montana. Even President Clinton and his family make Montana their favorite vacation spot.

Myrna Loy

Gary Cooper

Splendid Cities

Montana doesn't have any large cities. Montana is made up of small farming and **mining** towns. Even though the cities are small, each helps the state to prosper.

The largest city, Billings, has about 80,000 people. The city is a shipping and trade center. There are two colleges in Billings: Eastern Montana College and Rocky Mountain College.

In the city of Great Falls lives 55,000 people. This city lies on the Missouri River. Malmstrom Air Force Base is located in Great Falls. There are many farms in or around Great Falls.

Missoula, in the western part of the state, makes lumber and sends it to other places. It also is home to the University of Montana. Butte-Silver

Bow in the southwest has been famous for more than 100 years as a **mining** center. It has the World Museum of Mining.

Helena, the capital, stands in the Rockies just east of the Continental Divide. In southwestern Montana is Bozeman. Bozeman is a large farm and **ranch** region. It is also home to Montana State University. Many people visit Bozeman because Yellowstone National Park is nearby. It also has great mountain ski resorts.

Other splendid cities in Montana include, Kalispell, Havre, Miles City, Cardwell, Raidersburg, Choteau, Fairfield, Thompson Falls, Three Forks, Polson, and Hays.

The Capitol Building in Helena, Montana.

Montana's Land

The beautiful land of Montana is covered with mountains, lakes, rivers, and forests.

The Rocky Mountains are in the western area of Montana. In this area is the towering Lewis and Clark Range and the Absaroka Range, among others. In the Absaroka Range is Granite Peak, the highest point in the state.

In the northwest, where the Kootenai River crosses the Idaho border, is the lowest point in the state at 1,800 feet (549 m). This region also has the state's largest body of water, Flathead Lake.

The Missouri Plateau covers the rest of the state. It is more flat than other areas in the state, and much better for farming because of its rich soil. This region also has many rivers and lakes.

A mountain goat looking over a lake in Glacier National park, Montana.

Montana at Play

The people of Montana and the visitors to this wonderful state have many things to do. The beautiful national parks, dense forests, incredible mountains, and pleasant climate have made it a great place to play.

Tourism is one of Montana's fastest growing **industries**. The most popular attractions are Glacier and Yellowstone national parks.

Glacier National Park is joined with a Canadian national park. Since 1932, the combined parks have been officially known as Waterton-Glacier International Peace Park. Hundreds of years ago the Blackfeet **Native Americans** were so impressed by the beauty of this area that they set it aside as a sacred, special place.

Yellowstone National Park is visited even more. The canyons, geysers, waterfalls, petrified forests, and mountain scenery of the park make it one of the most awesome sights in the country.

In the Flathead Lake region, people fish and do watersports. There are mountain resorts for skiing, hiking, and mountain climbing. Dude **ranches**, ghost towns, and Montana's 11 national forests are also fun places to see.

Horseback riding is popular in Montana.

Montana at Work

The people of Montana must work to make money. The first **settlers** of Montana were fur traders. Later the gold rush took place and people made money by **mining** gold.

Today, the biggest **industries** are farming, mining, **manufacturing**, and **tourism**. The Treasure State has about 22,000 farms and **ranches**. Montana is third in producing wheat out of all the states. It is grown mostly on the eastern grasslands. Hay, barley, and oats are other major **crops**.

Many people in Montana work in the manufacturing industry. Most of this industry is based on its natural treasures. People make lumber and wood products out of trees that grow in the **vast** forests. They also make food products from the crops farmers grow.

Because so many people from around the world visit this scenic state, tourism is a big business. People work in service jobs. Service is cooking and serving food, working in stores, hotels, or restaurants.

The state of Montana has unbelievable beauty, wonderful people, and land filled with **minerals**. Because of this the Treasure State is a great place to visit, live, work, and play.

Logs floating downstream to be made into wood products.

MONTANA

Fun Facts

• In 1864, the Montana Territory was created and the capital was Bannack. The capital was then moved to Virginia City in 1865, and Helena in 1875—where it still is today.

• The cows outnumber the people in Montana about three to one.

• Montana is a very big state. Its land covers 145,388 square miles (376,553 sq km). It is the fourth biggest state.

• Montana's land covers a lot of area. From east to west the greatest distance is 559 miles (900 km). It would take over nine hours to drive across the state—that is without ever stopping!

Watching for grizzlies on Granite Peak.

Glossary

Crops: what farmers grow on their farm to either eat or sell.

Graze: animals eating grass.

Industry: many different types of businesses.

Manufacture: to make things by machine in a factory.

Minerals: things found in the earth, such as rock, diamonds, or coal.

Mining: working underground to get minerals.

Native Americans: the first people who were born in and occupied North America.

Natural gas: a type of gas that is found in the earth. It is used for fuel.

Petroleum: a oily, dark colored liquid that is found in the earth.

Ranching: like farming, but only animals are raised there, not any crops.

Settlers: people that move to a new land and build a community.

Tourism: an industry that serves people who are traveling for fun.

Vast: huge, widespread.

Internet Sites

Travel Montana
http://travel.mt.gov
This site has information on Montana attractions, events, recreation, camping, and more.

Montana Territories
http://www.montana.com
Montana Territories is information on resources from the great state of Montana. If you're thinking about visiting or moving to Montana, here is some information about some of our cities, towns, and natural resources.

Montana Information Source
http://www.mt-usa.com
An interactive website for Montana information. A database provides an easy way to find information on Montana residents and businesses by name, type, or location.

These sites are subject to change. Go to your favorite search engine and type in Montana for more sites.

PASS IT ON

Tell Others Something Special About Your State

To educate readers around the country, pass on interesting tips, places to see, history, and little unknown facts about the state you live in. We want to hear from you!

To get posted on ABDO & Daughters website E-mail us at "mystate@abdopub.com"

Index